Hamburger Hockey

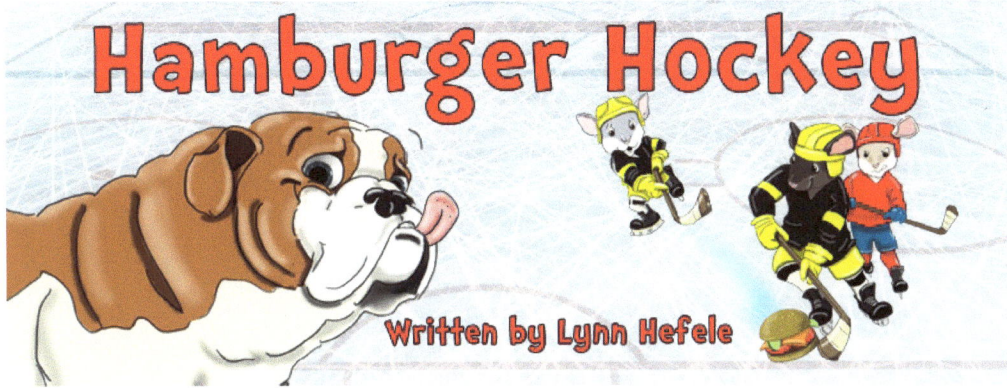

Written by Lynn Hefele

Hamburger Hockey

Manufactured in the United States of America
For information, please contact:
LEPE, Inc.
3 Griggs Drive
Greenlawn, NY 11740

www.LEPEinc.com
631-626-9190

ISBN-13: 978-0-9915008-8-8
LCCN: 2015901002
Illustrator contact information:
Steve McGinnis
http://www.digraphics.info/

Author contact information:
Lynn Hefele
lynn.hefele@gmail.com
Copyright © 2014

LEPE

Literature Enhanced Physical Education

To Marycatherine and Emma

"Jimmy, do you smell that?" asked Gloria.

"Of course I do!" Jimmy said, with his nose twitching out the door. "The smell of hamburger is like roses to me!"

"Hey, Trina, it looks like sliders!"
shouted Dad.

"Awesome, I'll get the sticks!"
replied Trina.

"Sneakers or skates?" asked Binky.
"Probably skates!   She's serving cranberry juice, again!"
answered her twin sister Pinky.

"Skipper, make sure you are wearing your helmet," doted Mom. "I know, I know, toss me my shoulder pads, please." whined Skipper.

"Those are my shin guards," yelled Zander.

"No, they're not!" screamed Niya yanking the pads out of her brother's hands.

"Pixie and Emmy, you two will be goalies today.   I'm going to be the referee," said Lorie as she put on her striped shirt.

Bam,

Bam,

Bam......

Splash!

"There it goes!" cheered Gloria.

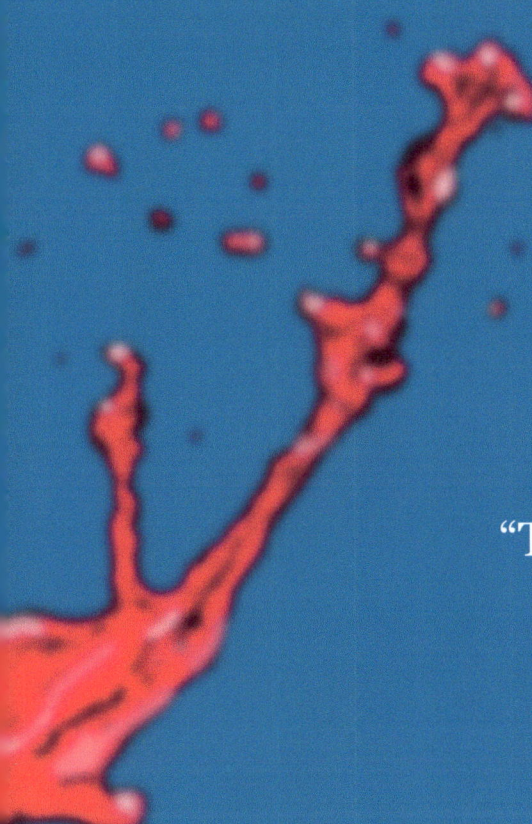

"She's cleaning him off," shouted Dad.
"She's mopping the floor!," yelled Zander.

"They're leaving the room," added Emmy.
"Game time!" Skipper squeaked.

The mice skated out to center ice and Lorie climbed up on the table. Gloria and Trina positioned themselves for the faceoff. Jimmy and Dad lined up on the left wing and Zander and Niya lined up on the right. Skipper and Mom, Pinky and Binky moved into the defensive positions while Pixie and Emmy skated back to protect the goals.

Each team would try to get the slider into the other team's hole. The team that scored the goal would get to split the slider. Lorie picked up the burger and let it drop.

20

Gloria won the faceoff and quickly began stick handling past Trina by tapping the slider with the inside and outside of her stick.

Skipper was fast to react and stole the hamburger puck and headed in the other direction.

After gliding past Jimmy, he passed the puck ahead to Zander who was guarded by Binky.

Zander weaved between the twins and with a quick snap of
the wrist sent the puck into the air toward the goal.
Pixie raised her glove to catch the puck but.........

Dog!!!!

Louie, the Keeshond, snatched the burger right out of the air and scurried out his doggie door, ending the first period.

Discouraged but hungry, both teams lined up for another face off and Lorie dropped the slider. This time Trina came away with the puck.

26

She snapped a pass to Dad. Jimmy, however, crossed in front
to steal the puck.

Jimmy slid between Skipper and Mom, hopped over a toy truck and approached the goal. He faked left and aimed for the top left corner of the hole.

28

The puck jumped off his stick and headed straight for Emmy,
but...

Dog!

Buckets, the Chocolate Labrador Retriever, barreled into the kitchen, snatched the burger right out of the air and scurried out the doggie door.

Lorie dropped the final slider to the ice and the mice battled back and forth for nearly 5 minutes until ......

Dogs!!!

Louie and Buckets crashed through the doggie door chased by Butchie the Bulldog!!!!

The mice scattered leaving Niya on a breakaway toward her
hole. She weaved around the table, through the legs of a
chair and lined up with the goal.

Niya brought her stick back for a slap shot as Louie, Buckets, and Butchie all bounded into the air to intercept the puck.

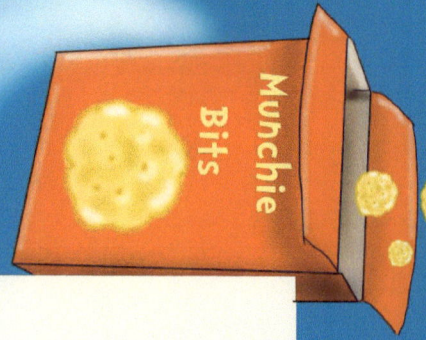

36

Crash!!!- went the dogs.

"Yippee!!!" cheered the mice.

Every mouse scurried back to his hole with a cracker carefully controlled.

Exhausted and full, Trina turned to her Dad and asked, "What do you think she'll make for dinner?" "I don't know," replied Dad, "but I hope it's meatballs."

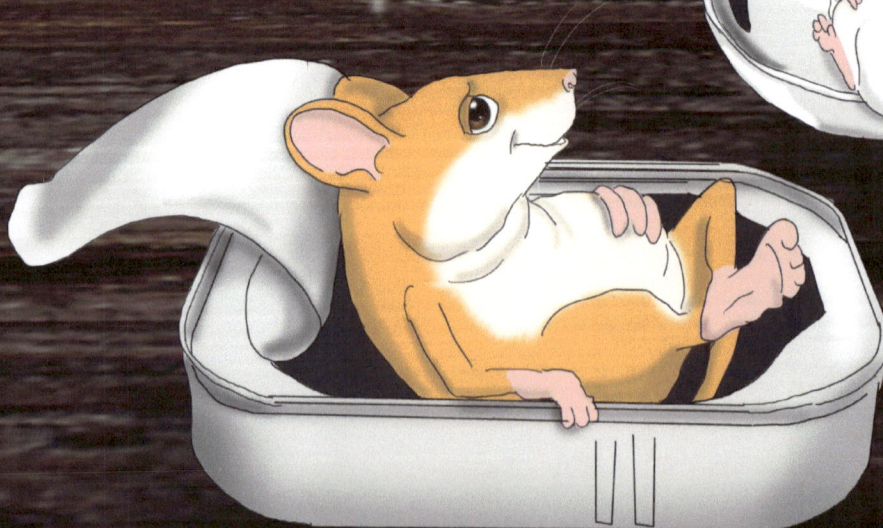